Hop on the Clue Bus

Hop on the Clue Bus

A Common Sense Guide to Leadership

By Heidy LaFleur
Foreword by Tom Keating
Cover Illustration by Garrett W. LaFleur

Copyright © 2015 Heidy J. LaFleur
All rights reserved.

ISBN: 0692403485
ISBN 13: 9780692403488
Library of Congress Control Number: 2015906758
Heidy LaFleur, Des Plaines, IL

A book like no other...

Hop on the Clue Bus
A Common Sense Guide to Leadership

Heidy LaFleur
Visit me at: Hoponthecluebus.com

Testimonials

What are teachers, leaders and parents saying about *Hop on the Clue Bus?*

Hop on the Clue Bus is a refreshing reminder to ALL educators that we have leaders in education who are still driven and compassionate. Heidy reminds us that we are ALL responsible for "leading" by the way we choose to lead our lives and treat one another. Whether we are serving as Principals, Department Chairs or simply teachers with a strong sense of mission, we can use these opportunities to help make the world of education a better place. It is up to us. Heidy gives us the encouragement and the tools to make this happen. She shares her Core Beliefs and demonstrates ways to implement them as a leader. She also reminds us to let our humanity show through AND provides teachers with language to help them articulate what THEY might need from THEIR leaders (because…. "It's all about the conversation.") Thank you, Heidy, for reminding all of us that Common Sense IS an acceptable resource in leadership that we DO have control over some things in life (ourselves and our dispositions) and that, together, we can accomplish ANYTHING. – Laura Dahl, Music Teacher

Testimonials

It's never been a tougher time in education with the demands put on schools and educators. As school leaders scramble to stay on top of all the new demands, sometimes they overlook the simple common sense leadership principles that truly work and make a difference in people's lives. Heidy's book, *Hop on the Clue Bus* is a thought-provoking guide to help any school leader become an effective leader of PEOPLE! We all know that leadership is affecting change in people, but how do you do it and get the results you want and need? Read Heidy's book and follow her simple steps to Common Sense Leadership and you will be on a journey to success. Get on the Bus and join others like Heidy in making a huge impact in students and teachers lives. Thanks Heidy for opening yourself up and sharing your own personal stories that are heartfelt, so we all can improve from your experience. -James Jones, MBA aka Jim "Basketball" Jones - National Youth Motivational Speaker and creator of We Are 1 Team Character Education Program

"I don't know how you do it." It's a statement that I hear all too often, from other teachers, from substitutes, from my peers. My work life is stressful, to say the least, not because of the environment or because I am not supported. It is simply due to all of the constant varying needs of my students. They are the students that I love, the students who make me crazy, the students who NEED me; they are the reason why I do it. There are days where I feel like maybe, quite possibly, I changed the world for the better. Then there are other days where I feel defeated. Those are the days when my all wasn't good enough. Maybe I could've done this, maybe this would've worked instead. On those days, I fall into my chair at my desk at the end of the day, and there in front of me is a tattered post-it

Testimonials

note that reads, "You are amazing!" –Heidy. That is exactly the reminder I need. Heidy thinks that I am amazing. So I don't care that today I feel like I failed. Tomorrow she expects me to be back here and continue to be amazing. It's this feeling of being defended that Heidy brings. She sticks up for what she feels is right, and very eloquently, puts her stylish foot down and declares that she will not tolerate anything or anyone trying to put down her teachers, staff or mission for our school. This is an admirable trait that not many have. She is loyal and honest and hilarious, but most importantly, she is a person, just like the rest of us. When I think of Heidy, the first thing that comes to my mind is "she gets it." She understands our classroom. I don't know how she manages to support a school, deal with everyone's problems and still manage to be positive, funny and realistic. She loves her school and her staff. She makes it look so easy. *Hop on the Clue Bus* <u>IS</u> Heidy. It is her sense of humor, it is her philosophy, and it is her actions. These are the things that she does every day and has found great success. I am honored to be a part of her school. -Denise Rubio, Paraprofessional

Heidy has nailed it. This book is absolutely the most effective way to run a school and to live your life! As a social worker, I teach students that they can always adjust their attitude when there is a problem situation. It is truly amazing to have a leader who is always able to find the positives in situations and people. Living this way, Heidy has created an environment where people want to come to work. It is nice to know that we are supported by her and that she is here to help us grow in our weak areas (because we all have them). If more people used Common Sense and "Hopped on the Clue Bus" the world would be a better place. – Elisabeth Betancourt, School Social Worker

Testimonials

This is a sensational, motivational and thought-provoking book that will serve as an inspiration to anyone lucky enough to read it! This is not only a guide for everyday work, but for everyday life. – Judy Mendoza, Abigail's mom

There is something magical about Heidy. Driving Heidy's leadership qualities are faith, hope and love. Heidy speaks of her love and compassion for her staff, students and families that she serves. I remember the hope that Heidy inspired as she broke down the Danielson rubric a year before our district adopted the model. She observed every teacher on specific points of the rubric and provided feedback and growth discussions. We, teachers, had a stress-free year long trial run. What amazing leadership! I had no idea of the heights I would grow with Heidy at the wheel. Her faith in me and in her staff provided us with the security to try new things and augment the rigor of our classrooms. –Susana Poppe, ELL Teacher

Thanks for being this principal and person Heidy - your coach nailed it in that letter, it was beautiful.... – Jason Osterlund, 5th grade teacher

Get ready for a truly inspiring ride! In this book, Heidy LaFleur provides AWESOME insight into what makes a person into a positive, productive and successful leader. Heidy reminds us that common sense NEEDS to play a role in leadership because it helps to shape the teams we lead. A ride on the "Clue Bus" will not soon be forgotten because the lessons you learn along the way will enhance your thinking and will make you a more effective and encouraging leader!
- Sarah Mueller, Kindergarten Teacher

Testimonials

From the years of 2007–2012, Mrs. LaFleur was the Assistant Principal at my children's elementary school. I was immediately drawn to the strength and kindness that illuminated from her. During the time she served at our school, she always had such an approachable demeanor. Whether you found yourself next to her on the playground, or needed a seat in her office, she was always available with a willingness to not only listen, but with an eagerness to work to resolve whatever issue may be at hand. Her commitment to each child at our school was so evident, she wasn't just an administrator with a title, she was one with us. For me personally, my children faced both classroom struggles and personal heartbreak. During those times, Mrs. LaFleur was always a beacon of compassion, thoughtfulness, and encouragement to not only them, but to me as well. Our lives have been blessed with the gift of Heidy LaFleur. -Deana Rife, Noah & Skylar's mom

Heidy is a truly amazing leader. Her positive attitude, compassion and determination are contagious! She is the perfect person to educate and inspire other leaders. *Hop on the Clue Bus* is filled with examples of what awesome leaders possess and ideas that can easily be implemented immediately. *Hop on the Clue Bus* is a must read for every leader looking to improve their leadership skills and strengthen their team. Thank you Heidy for reflecting upon past experiences, taking notes along the way, and sharing your leadership toolbox; your book will change so many lives! -Amy D'Antonio, Special Education

Dedication

This book is dedicated to my husband Garrett for his unconditional love, support, guidance and friendship. Now that this book is complete, our house may be clean again!
I love you always & forever. Man, are we lucky!

To my beautiful children Lilly, Garrett & Peter - You are so magical to me and I love you more than you could ever imagine.

To my amazing sisters, Katy & Greta…She would be proud of us and who we have become.

To my charismatic nephew Cordell…Like grandma said, "Just look at him Heidy. He is going to be something special." She was right.

The Bus Route

Bus Stop 1 - Climate & Frustration 1

Bus Stop 2 - Shh, Listen! 9

Bus Stop 3 - Communication & Motivation 15

Bus Stop 4 - High Expectations with Human Touch 21

Bus Stop 5 - Compassion 27

Bus Stop 6 - Organization 33

Bus Stop 7 - Evaluation 39

Bus Stop 8 - Relationships 43

Bus Stop 9 - It's Up to You 47

Foreword

Every so often, the stars align just right and I am able to enjoy a chance "reunion" with someone who has a special place in my heart. On March 14th of this year, I was fortunate enough to reconnect with Heidy Pemsl at the Iowa State Boys Basketball Tournament where Heidy was watching her nephew compete for a state title. Our brief conversation reminded me of how this incredible woman has impacted me in such a positive way and has helped me develop my own professional qualities.

My relationship with Heidy goes back to the early 1990's when I coached her in volleyball at Wahlert High School in Dubuque. It was clear even then that there was something very special about her. She was, in every sense of the word, a "leader."

It comes as no surprise that Heidy has authored an outstanding book on leadership. Through my own experience as an athlete, teacher, coach, athletic director and now principal of a high school, I've been blessed to have interacted with some truly outstanding leaders. Through those interactions, I've come to my own understanding of

Foreword

the essence of leadership. For as long as I've known her, Heidy has exemplified those qualities.

Heidy is, in the truest sense of the term, a "servant leader." She has always taken responsibility for those she has led. As captain of our volleyball team her senior year, she willed to the state tournament a team that "on paper" had no business competing for any kind of championship. She did it by sending a message loud and clear to her teammates that she believed in each and every one of them and that she would do whatever it took to help them develop into the kind of competitors who could indeed vie for championships. Because she believed in them, they believed in her.

A bona fide leader leads by example and leads with integrity. This was simply part of Heidy's DNA. She never expected anything from others – her coaches, her teachers, her teammates, her friends, her family – that she did not expect of herself. If she wanted greater effort from teammates, she ramped up her own effort (which was off the charts already!). If she wanted a positive environment, she created it with her own enthusiasm and encouragement. We could always count on Heidy to do the right thing – whether anyone was watching or not – simply because it was the right thing to do.

A leader shares the gifts he or she has been blessed with. Heidy believed that it was her responsibility to use her athletic ability not for personal accolades but for the success of her teams. More importantly, she used it to simply not allow her teammates to fail. Whether it was running down an errant pass, finding a way to attack a less than perfect set or launching her body toward the floor to dig a ball that got by a block, her teammates knew that Heidy "had their back."

A critical element of leadership is humility. Even as a teenager, Heidy knew the importance of directing compliments away from herself and toward her teammates. She realized that opponents deserved praise for their performances and for challenging her and her teammates. In a world of swag and chest-thumping, Heidy was a breath of fresh air.

Most importantly, the best leaders I've encountered lead from a position of unconditional love. Whether a teacher who loves students, a coach who loves athletes, a director who loves performers or a captain who loves teammates, the true leader feels an emotional connection to those he or she leads. There was never any doubt that Heidy's leadership was, at its core, a demonstration of love for those she led. We could hear it in her voice. We could see it in her eyes. We could feel it in her touch.

True leaders understand that, "it's not about them." They focus their efforts on others. The true leader takes great satisfaction in the accomplishments of those they lead. I saw Heidy experience the exhilaration of conference and state championships earned. But the joy I witnessed when her teammates succeeded – individually and collectively – was something to behold.

I am so happy that Heidy has chosen to share her "common sense" guide to leadership with the world. Her perspective is one that will benefit all of us and if we take her words to heart, will benefit those

Foreword

we have been called to lead. From the moment I met her, I have grown to love Heidy Pemsl for the phenomenal human being she is. After reading, *Hop on the Clue Bus*, you'll understand why.

Tom Keating, Principal
Xavier High School

Preface

It seems that in some places of work and life, people are happy, willing, positive and productive. Yet in other places, people are miserable, unmotivated, frustrated and noncompliant. I used to wonder why some people were such complainers and so unhappy. Why is it, I thought, that the majority of people I'm with are excited to work hard and motivated to share both their strengths and weaknesses with me? I have found that on every team I've been on and at every job I have had, people have come to me for help, understanding, guidance and reassurance. As I reflect on my career thus far, it all comes down to loving people, listening to people and finding ways to lift people to their highest potential. As the years have come and gone, and I have worked with different leaders, I have learned that leadership is magical. Magical leaders make people want to work. Magical leaders are looked up to for advice, strength and approval. Magical leaders are consistent. Magical leaders strike a balance between fun and high expectations. Magical leaders are not afraid to show that they are human and make mistakes. Magical leaders laugh. Magical leaders follow through…always.

I want to say that magical leadership is common sense, but I have realized that common sense is not very common. Some leaders are selfish. Some are worried about things other than people. Some leaders are worried too much about what others think of them. Some leaders are worried about money. Some will walk all over others to get to the top. Some leaders look down upon people while preaching from up top and worst of all, is when politics lead the leadership. Ugh.

However, some live by the MOST IMPORTANT three "P's" and three "C's."

POSITIVE
    PRODUCTIVE
        PROBLEM SOLVER
            CHEMISTRY
                CULTURE
                    CHARACTER

Think about it. The leaders, bosses, principals and coaches, who genuinely hold the "P's" and "C's" closely, <u>find success.</u> It's all about people. It's about finding strengths in individual people and making them into a team. Period.

I have been blessed with leaders in my life from which I have taken notes on things I have put in my leadership tool box. Thank you, mom for making me believe I was the best and that I could do anything. I know you are looking down on me every day with a proud smile. Thank you, Mr. Mac, for telling me in 2nd grade that I was the best kickball player in the world. Thank you, Mr. Draus, for moving me into the Blue Dolphins high reading group because you said I was ready for a challenge. Thank you, Mrs. Wilgenbush, for having such high expectations in junior high that we were afraid to let you down. Thank you, Mr. Keating, for coaching us to two state championships and demanding nothing but the very best at every practice, every game and in the classroom. You made us believe that there was no one that was going to beat us. Thank you, Mr. Sampson, for being on my side when the going got tough junior year. Thank you, Coach, for putting me in the varsity game as a freshman in the bottom on the 9th inning being down 2-0 with 2 outs. I struck out, but I took notes. Thank you, as well, for taking me out of the clean-up spot in the lineup after I broke the home run record. I didn't understand, but I took notes. Thank you, Coach, for making us weigh in after you fed us pizza and yelled out our weight in front of the football players telling us that we were all too fat. I was angry, but I took notes. Thank you, Assistant Principal, for making up my observations and not providing me with any opportunity to talk about my growth as a teacher. I survived but I took notes. Thank you, Principal, for writing me up as a teacher for having a coffee pot in my room, even though I didn't drink coffee and it was the teacher next door to me. I was bummed, but I took notes. Thank you, other Principal, for giving me a needs improvement in attendance because I only achieved 95% the year my mother was dying of cancer. I was scared, but I took notes. Thank you, large school district, for creating a program for principals that sent me through tests and interviews and said I wasn't qualified to be a principal. After 14 years of excellent service to kids and colleagues, you chewed me up and spit me out, but I took notes.

I have learned from the most magical leaders and from among the worst leaders ever. From each, I have taken notes along the way and developed my own style of magic that is based on **common**

sense and I would like to share it with all of you. So come on…Hop on the Clue Bus with me! Bring your friends! Don't forget, the cool kids sit in the back. The Clue Bus is a great place to be!

Heidy LaFleur

I hope my achievements in life shall be these…that I will have fought for what was right and fair, that I will have risked for that which mattered, that I will have given help to those who were in need…that I have left the earth a better place for what I've done and who I've been.   - C. Hoppe

Acknowledgements

I am forever grateful to those who encouraged me.

Thank you GB for creating such an amazing cover image. When I asked you to draw me a clue bus, you sparked such creativity and I just love it!

Thank you Lilly for writing such a beautiful paragraph about your mother!

Thank you Peter for making me laugh every day!

Thank you Natalie Biancalana, Hal Shepherd and Katy Pemsl for spending so much time editing for me.

Thank you Coach Keating, for writing such a powerful foreword.

Thank you to all colleagues from all parts of my career who shared their beliefs of what you see in effective leaders. Your sincere words will help leaders all over the world.

Thank you to Judy and Shannon for allowing me to use your daughters' inspirational stories in my book.

Thank you to Amy, Elisabeth, Deana, Denise, Jason, Jim, Judy, Laura, Sarah & Susana for reading my book in its early stages and writing testimonials.

Support LIVE LIKE LEAH - http://www.livelikejohn.org/leah/

Hop on the Clue Bus

NO REALLY, PLEASE GET ON.

<u>Our work involves being and modeling these people:</u>

Ms. Positive   Mr. Productive   Mrs. Problem Solver

<u>Our work involves creating and guiding these people:</u>

Mrs. Chemistry   Mr. Culture   Ms. Character

Hop on the Clue Bus

If you don't have these people in your school, it's another reason to get on the bus!

With common sense and the right attitude,

you can do anything.
you can lead anyone.
you **will** find success.

Introduction

The idea sparked as I sat, nine months pregnant, in my final master's class back in 2003. We were discussing teacher evaluation and I started to jot notes. In my head, I thought many things:

"Are you serious?"
"Oh my God. You are clueless."
"This guy will never make it."
"What is going on here?"

You see, my classmates were sharing their views on teachers, on people. My whole life had been spent on teams and developing skills to deal with all different kinds of people. I was a problem solver and obsessed with finding success not only for myself, but for those surrounding me. I was hearing people talk about how easy leadership was and how a top-down approach is always best. Like many times then and now, I sat back and observed. I listened. I took notes. I imagined what my school would be like. I dreamed about helping teachers and kids and couldn't wait. I heard my beautiful mother telling me, "Oh Heidy, what a bunch of nitwits." There were so many classmates who didn't seem to understand that leadership is all about people. Leadership IS about organization, management, motivation,

Introduction

expectations, relationships and the growth **of PEOPLE**. During that class, one of the things I jotted in my notebooks was, "These people need to get a clue," and that is where the title was born.

As professionals and leaders, we read so much on research & theory and all of it is relevant and important in developing our philosophies. I always felt, however, that we were missing discussion on common sense. Someday, I would love to create and teach a Common Sense Leadership course in college. What a perfect addition it would be to School Finance, Leaders as Change Agents and Leadership & Organization. Imagine a course that would help you make all of those better because you understand people. For example, you can talk to someone who knows a million leadership theories, but isn't an effective leader. Some will study and do well in school, but in the real world they flounder. I often asked myself what was it that I felt was missing from all of my classes. I remember sitting in some classes thinking, "Ah, this is such bullshit. What is it really like?" Well, this book will tell you what it's really like. It will tell you the importance of common sense and taking care of people. It will tell you how difficult conversations and honesty will make your team stronger. It will tell you that the most respected leaders put people first, talk the talk AND walk the walk. Respected and effective leaders honor people, guide people and listen to people. Never mistake this "soft" approach as weakness. In fact, this approach is difficult and draining at times, but worth every minute.

Just as a principal must lead teachers, teachers must lead students. All of the leadership qualities of effective leaders are the same in the classroom with teachers. The teachers who have the greatest impact on students are those who build relationships with their kids. They get to know them and help them grow. They do what it takes to understand how to motivate them, guide them and help them find success in and out of the classroom. What teachers do you remember? I remember the teachers who cared about me as not only Heidy the student, but as Heidy the child, adolescent, teenager and young adult. I remember the teachers who asked me about a game, about colleges, about my life. I know they taught me academics, but those who made a true impact went way beyond fractions and diagramming sentences. This, to me, is the difference in life. Each one of us has the ability to make life a little easier for someone else; because God knows life can be very difficult.

I often wonder where some of those classmates are today. I bet some are great leaders and some aren't so effective. Those who are respected and making progress are on the bus. They get it. Who are the leaders in your life that you respect? What is it about them that you respect? On the other side of the token, why are some of you miserable, frustrated and held back? I will leave you with that question because this is something WE ALL have in common. People are interesting and those on the bus will lift you up and make you want to work hard. Those not on the bus, piss you off and make your life difficult. For all of you, my wish is that you get to experience second-to-none leadership and you are lifted up and honored in the work you do. I also wish for leaders everywhere, to take a step back and reflect on how you could make someone's life a little easier...

All the Best,
Heidy

I
Climate & Frustration

CLUE BUS NOTE #1

If it feels good in the moment, don't say it!

[in-san-i-tee] <u>insanity</u>: noun - the condition of being insane; a derangement of the mind & a foolish or senseless action, policy, statement, etc.

You are in control. You are in control of your thoughts and your mind. You are in control of your attitude and the way you present yourself to others. You are in control of how you treat people and how much time you devote to people. Is the glass half empty or half full? As a common sense leader, I know that my outlook and attitude control the climate of my school.

You may wonder why I'm beginning at the bus stop on frustration, but common sense tells us that we all feel it. The positive

Climate & Frustration

leaders, the negative leaders, the common sense leaders all experience levels of frustration! When you feel, as a leader, that you are drowning in work and you feel like you have no control about what is happening in your school or in your life, it is beyond frustrating. When I was a kid, I thought that as I got older, things would get easier. Ha! I remember starting my teaching career and telling myself it would be easier the longer I taught and that by the time I was 40, I would have it all figured out. I laugh at myself, but also enjoy the innocence in that train of thought. I am very close to turning 40 and I haven't figured it all out. But here is what I know:

I have learned that life is a roller coaster. It's so fun AND so scary. It's so easy AND so hard. We all go through some great times and we all go through tough times. All people will go through something really difficult. It's not a matter of if; it's a matter of when. Some of the things that get us through both are family, friends and our attitude. The only common factor among the three is attitude. Some of us don't have a lot of family or friends, but we all have an attitude. Common sense leadership helps me remind others that at school and in life, peoples' attitudes are developed by their surroundings. **We have so much power as leaders to form the attitude and actions of others.** It takes time, but it is possible to help develop the positive in people. Positive people create a successful, thriving climate. The more positive support I spread as a leader, the more people will follow me...The more we will get done...The more effectively we develop children to their fullest potential.

When I'm frustrated it's my responsibility to pull it together for myself and those around me. My attitude guides me. I just have to get through the moment. When speaking while frustrated, I find it extremely important to remember that I have no idea what someone may be going through. A mentor once told me to never quit my job in the spring because frustration hits hard when school is about to end each year. He also reminded me that when frustrated, I may be tempted to say something that feels great in the moment and will be regretted an hour later. His advice was, ***"Be smart and if it feels good in the moment, don't say it!"***

Working in a large urban district for fourteen years brought a great deal of frustration, but I took notes. I worked my butt off as a fourth grade teacher. I stayed late. I created rigorous plans. I wrote my own assessments. I had positive growth results with my students, but I was still frustrated. A few years after I started, my principal asked me to teach sixth and seventh grade math and I accepted the challenge. I prepared by studying student data, I formed groups, facilitated learning with guided note taking and grew kids in math, yet the parents received a letter stating that I was not "highly qualified." Seriously? Ask the students, the parents, my principal and my colleagues if I was highly qualified. They are the ones who will be able to tell you. I learned that what mattered most was my preparation, planning and attitude; not the politics. #Frustrated

A few years later, I accepted the assistant principal position at the same school. I was so ready and excited. I now felt that I could not only help shape a classroom of 30 students, but a whole school of teachers. My mission was to get into the classrooms and be a true instructional leader. What would be better than helping teachers be the best teachers they can be? I was motivated to guide and help

Climate & Frustration

lower achieving teachers either along the road to improvement, or to move them out. ***If you've had the opportunity to observe poor instruction, you know what I mean.*** Too often, people don't exhibit the courage to have those tough conversations with teachers who struggle. Common sense tells us that if they are struggling, they may be doing harm in the classroom. I have the responsibility to help them improve. I also have the responsibility to work on getting them out if the help is not enough. Kids get one shot at school and we all need to be at the top of our game. As a mother, I can't say enough about my children's teachers. Some have been unbelievable and others, well let's just say they are lucky not to be working in my building. Again, those of you who have had your children spend a year with a less than superior teacher know what I mean. For those who haven't seen poor instruction, don't worry, you will, and I challenge you to provide as much guidance as possible. If it doesn't work - do what you have to do to get excellent teachers in front of kids. The climate of your school will grow strong if you support those who excel and mentor those in need. Your climate will grow even stronger and more respectful if you follow through with tough conversations and hold people accountable to offer the best for kids.

In the school, our principal was overwhelmed with requests from the district, budget deadlines, faxes that came in with due dates of three days ago, changing leadership and conflicting philosophies. She was never able to go into the classrooms and be a true instructional leader. Though not her fault, we were on our own. Common sense would say that putting insane demands on a principal of a school and expecting amazing results is silly. Common sense would say that cramming 30 or more students into a classroom and expecting all kids to learn is ridiculous. Common sense would say that changing philosophy, CEOs, and expectations will not keep people above water. Common sense tells us that when the demand is greater than the supply, things are not going to get done well. ***It's frustrating to be a part of that, but again, we have control of our attitude and actions.***

When I was a senior in high school, I was the only returning starter on both the Varsity volleyball and basketball teams. Mr. Keating asked a former player, Kari Hamel, for some advice and she said – Be a part of the solution, not a part of the problem. Mr. Keating shared that with me and I share it everywhere I go. It is amazing advice. It is very simple. If you change your perspective, anything is possible. I came across the note he wrote me and I'd like to share it with you:

> All The Way To State!
>
> Heidy,
> Early this year I told you that Kari Hamel said it was important for you to be part of the solution, not part of the problem. You took those words to heart and have helped us get to where we are today. You have been a patient and supportive leader. You have been a heck of a player. Let's put it together one more time and get back to State!
> Coach K.
>
> Hey! Hey!
> Whatta Ya Say?

Mr. Keating took the time to write a note to appreciate and motivate me. Things like this truly make a difference. He certainly made a difference in my life.

Climate & Frustration

It's a choice – be a part of the solution or be a part of the problem. Things can be very frustrating at times and God knows some of our buildings have poor leadership, but do what you can to be a part of the solution. I will keep working on the poor leadership part...I will save more seats on the bus for those in need!

I was very fortunate to work at an <u>AMAZING</u> school in a large urban district. The staff and families were wonderful. The students were eager to learn and brought such joy to the school community. It's unfortunate that this district gets such a bad name at times, because there are so many <u>AMAZING people</u> doing so many <u>AMAZING things</u> with children.

In order to drive through the frustration that comes with leadership and life, I live by a quote from C. Hoppe. This quote reminded me how to deal with the bureaucracy of large entities and continues to help me each and every day:

> I hope my achievements in life shall be these...
> that I will have fought for what was right and fair,
> that I will have risked for that which mattered,
> that I will have given help to those who were in
> need...that I have left the earth a better place for
> what I've done and who I've been. - C. Hoppe

Regardless of the frustration that educational regulations - No Child Left Behind, Common Core, PARCC - can bring, I am the Master of my Fate and the Captain of my Soul. It is my job to help teachers help kids every day. It doesn't matter what the latest mandate is. Help them grow. End of story.

The politics of education will always be there, *but we have control over how we deal with it.* No one can take away what we do in schools and in classrooms with students each day. I find honor in the fact that my words and actions shape the culture which shapes the climate of the school. I find honor in helping teachers be the best they can be. I find honor in open and honest conversations. Mostly, I find honor in opening up and allowing people into my life so they are never growing as educators next to a stranger.

Beginning my college student/athlete experience as a Division I volleyball player, I was overcome with frustration. I learned a whole lot of what not to do in leadership. I went from a State Championship and nationally-ranked high school program of belief and power, to a college program of put-downs, outrageous workouts and negativity. When I arrived as a freshman, the seniors were burned out before pre-season began. At our first team dinner, one of the seniors came to me and asked if I was homesick. I told her I was and she said, "Well good luck, because at this place it doesn't get any better." Yikes. How could she have said that? What kind of climate was I walking into? I was positive and ready. I wasn't going to get beat by anyone and I was a winner...or so I thought. The coach made fun of me because I was Catholic. What? What was wrong with that? That's all I knew coming from Dubuque, Iowa. *If you grew up in Dubuque, Iowa, you will know exactly what I mean!* She would talk about girls' bodies and make fun of people on our team. There was no vision. There was no cohesive unit. There was no motivation. It was brutal. After three-hour conditioning practices, we would have to run a mile in under seven minutes or we had to do it again. It was by the grace of God that I ran that thing under seven minutes every time. She would then make us weigh in and if she didn't like what the scale said, we would work out more. I certainly wish I was as "fat" now as I was then!

    I didn't have the motivation to impress. None of it made sense to me. There was no focus on team or individual growth. I didn't have the drive to make her proud because it didn't matter. It felt horrible. For three years, I continued to tell myself, however, that I wasn't going to feel or act like the seniors did. Although I tried very hard, four years later it happened. I just wanted to get out and be done. A sport that I loved and was so passionate about had become a chore. Facing that leader on a daily basis was enough to make me nauseous. There was no vision. There was no plan. There was no pride. I learned a lot from her. Never lead without a backbone. Listen to your people. Believe in them and get to know them. Make them feel like they are on top of the world and they will work hard for you. Common sense tells us that frustration comes in many forms, and as leaders, we have the power to make everything palatable for our teachers. ***It's all in the presentation.*** The presentation is very powerful.

    I left college with a sour taste, determined to make a difference with people…

II
Shhh, Listen!

CLUE BUS NOTE # 2

Guiding people is VERY powerful if done with a people-first attitude.

[lee-der-ship] leadership: noun - the position or function of a leader, a person who guides or directs a group

Those of us blessed with the sense of hearing should know that listening is one of the most powerful things in the world. ***Hiring the right people and <u>investing the time to listen to them</u> is crucial to begin or continue your common sense journey.*** I enjoy interviewing teacher candidates because I learn so many things by listening to what they share with me. Interviews, to me, are one of the best times to sit back and learn about people. I learn about what other schools are doing to move their schools and their students forward. I also hear the brutal mistakes schools are making and wonder to myself, wow, what are people thinking? I learn about how people act when they are anxious and under pressure. I learn, through listening, how positive and productive individuals are. I learn if they can be problem solvers. Think about the difference you can make at an interview. As a leader, you can drill questions and expect to hear what you want to hear or you can sit at the table together and allow the candidate to discuss and share their value. Every person has something to offer and you should take mental notes as you interview. You never know when someone else's words will come in handy. One of my very favorite interviews ended with a young woman telling me that she just needed a chance to show what she can do. I really liked her and her style. She shared many wonderful ideas on how she grew not only students, but staff. I was the one who gave her that chance. She is an effective teacher today and we often talk about her quote at the end of the interview, "I just need someone to give me a chance." I'm glad I listened.

Working in a school setting with adults and children provides numerous opportunities to listen. Magical leaders listen with their entire bodies. They get on their hands and knees with kindergarten students and sit knee to knee with teachers and parents. They take their desk out of the equation to remove the barrier that separates the hierarchy of position. Magical leaders take time for people, listen to people and allow people time to be heard. They take time for parents too. Sometimes when a parent comes in screaming injustice regarding their child, they just want someone to listen. Some leaders start fuming and get into a battle of words. Magical leaders take a deep breath and know that the parent is frustrated, upset and needs an outlet. Sometimes as leaders, that is exactly what we are. We are an outlet for students, teachers and parents. I'm not saying it's easy to take, or listen to, I'm just saying it's a common sense fact.

Leaders are honored when things are going well and blamed when things go poorly. Magical leaders stay the course, listen to their players and take mental notes. They devise a plan **with the input of the team** in order to achieve success. *Listening to your team is one of the most effective outcomes of common sense leadership.* Your teams of teachers are in the classrooms, with the students all day. <u>Who could possibly know more about what needs to happen and suggest how to make things happen?</u> As a common sense leader, you will learn a lot about your teachers if you listen to them. Some of their input you will seek right away, some of their input will be put on a shelf for later and some of their input you will simply ignore. But the fact is, you listened. If people feel valued, they will work hard. If people know you genuinely listen to them, they will work hard. To me, this is common sense, but it isn't to everyone.

In all of my experiences, I have come to the common sense conclusion that if we not only listen, but listen well, it will make a world of difference. People have great ideas. People want feedback. The vast majority of people work so hard and want to succeed. It seems that many decisions are made without thoughtful listening and planning. We are surrounded with expertise. Shh, just listen. We are surrounded with people who are ready for the next step. Shh, just listen. <u>Magical leaders find strength in EVERY team member and put them to work.</u> *Finding strength in your team means that you paid attention to them and listened to them.* It works...I promise!

Shhh, Listen!

Too many times I have seen leaders make decisions without consulting with other team members. Common sense tells us that successful teams talk together and respect each other's work. As leaders, we have what it takes to make that happen. We lead it. We facilitate it. We participate and praise it. Over time, our teachers will see that we have been listening. It is amazing when it all comes together. In a smoothly run system, people feel valued and heard. People feel safe to take risks. People are grateful, motivated and determined to do their best. They are there, just listen to them.

Unless I have a confidential phone call or meeting, my door is literally open...always. Teachers know they are welcome to come in and talk and I will listen. They also know that if they come in with a complaint, that I expect they include a possible solution. That allows us to problem solve together. If you have an issue with something, it's fine by me, but know that I will expect that you share a way to solve the problem. Common sense even comes from Sesame Street...two heads are better than one.

In Illinois, teachers are soon to be partially evaluated on student growth. What a time to listen! Many are worried about the unknown and how this will be calculated! Many want to share their frustrations and areas of growth. What a time to listen. When the culture of a school has been established, people will come and share their worries with you. The best thing about my job is that I get to help them grow in their teaching, which will have a dramatic impact on children. The first step to helping teachers grow is listening to them. Listening to people will lead to great things and help you make decisions to push your school to the top.

Listening to others isn't always an easy thing. Sometimes I feel like I help solve everyone's problems and it's exhausting. I think, man, I have enough issues in my life to worry about. However, I truly try to live by the C. Hoppe quote. I do all that it takes to make each day the best it can be so when it's time to bow out of this life, I will be able to do so with pride and integrity that I did all I could do to make things right.

Take the time to listen to people; it will make a difference...

III

Communication & Motivation

CLUE BUS NOTE # 3

I see it. I see what I want it to look like. I match my actions to my sight.

[vizh-*uh* n] vision: noun - the act or power of anticipating that which will or may come to be

There's nothing like trying to get somewhere without a map. It never works very well. One of the most crucial elements of common sense leadership is that you need a map and you must share it with your teachers. Open communication will keep everyone out of the dark. The dark is a very scary place to be when you are looking for guidance. If a leader doesn't know where he/she is going, then the followers will have no clue. Having no clue leads to frustration, anger and resentment...three things that can ruin school culture very quickly.

Communication & Motivation

As a leader, having vision of where you want to take your school is one thing, but actually communicating that vision to others is another. ***Common sense leadership is developing your vision and talking about it all of the time.*** Everything that happens in your school must be driven by the vision. If a clear vision has been established and communicated, your teachers will know where they are going. They will work hard and focus on that vision because they are reminded through your verbal and written communication that it is at the forefront of decision-making. Your actions as a leader will motivate them to be the very best they can be. Common sense tells us that motivation comes from both within each of us AND from what our leaders tell us & how they treat us. I believe that if someone is doing well, they should hear it from me. Successful leaders send motivational emails, notes, cards and sometimes even small gifts. If teachers know that you see their efforts, they will believe in your vision and work hard. I also believe that when teachers aren't living up to my expectations, I need to do the same. Sending a note, a card or an email reminding the teacher of our vision and offering a hand or an ear can go a very long way in making sure the entire team is on the same page. Words are very powerful. Communication is key. ***Common sense leaders communicate when things are going beautifully AND when things are slipping.***

I will always remember the week before every high school volleyball match; Mr. Keating would give us the scouting report. He created a document showing the rotation of players of the team we were playing. In each rotation, he would tell us what the team was doing and where we could attack. He shared percentages of where their hitters hit and where they served. He matched our line-up to best meet theirs and repeated his vision over and over. <u>We were</u>

prepared. The vision of Wahlert High School volleyball was that we were going to win - hands down. Through his verbal and written communication, we believed that we worked harder, we practiced harder and we were going to win every match - no questions asked. Mr. Keating was organized. He had a vision. He lived it. He communicated it. He made us believe and it worked.

In the 1992 State Volleyball Championship in Cedar Rapids, Iowa, I was a sophomore starter and we were playing Hull Western Christian in the championship match. We knew the vision. We were prepared and confident that the vision would be sealed that night. Little did we know that we would be down two games to none in a very short time. I remember a few of the upperclassmen getting so upset on the court. They were saying that the refs did not want us to win because all of the calls were going against us. They were hitting balls way out of bounds and serving into the net. Our team was losing sight of the vision. All that we had worked for was slowly blurring and unfamiliarity was overcoming us. I had never been part of something so important to me and it felt like it was slipping away.

After the second match, we ran into the locker room and sat down. No one said much and the pit in my stomach grew bigger. My teammates had their heads down and I had never seen that before. Mr. Keating usually came in all fired up either telling us to get our heads out of our butts or praising us to continue in the manner that we were. This time was different. The communication he used was among the most powerful I have ever experienced. He took our blurred minds and refocused us by uniquely sharing the vision we lived by.

Communication & Motivation

Mr. Keating walked calmly into the locker room and said:

> Out of the night that covers me,
> Black as the pit from pole to pole,
> I thank whatever gods may be
> For my unconquerable soul.
>
> In the fell clutch of circumstance
> I have not winced nor cried aloud.
> Under the bludgeonings of chance
> My head is bloody, but unbowed.
>
> Beyond this place of wrath and tears
> Looms but the Horror of the shade,
> And yet the menace of the years
> Finds and shall find me unafraid.
>
> It matters not how strait the gate,
> How charged with punishments the scroll,
> I am the master of my fate,
> I am the captain of my soul.

He was passionate. He was real. He was communicating that we were in control of our fate. After reciting William Ernest Henley's *Invictus*, he looked each of us in the eye and said, "If we are going down tonight, it better be with the best fight you have in you," and he walked out. We all stood up, looked at each other and came together in a circle. Someone said, "Let's go. Let's do this." We ran back out onto that court and won the next three games winning the

Communication & Motivation

State Championship. The match ended with me serving two aces to the front row. I went on to serve a million more balls in my career, but never in my life have I experienced such poise and confidence while serving a ball as I did that magical night.

Mr. Keating's way of motivating us that evening is proof that the way a leader communicates is vital to the outcome. In a school, we strive for students to grow socially, emotionally and academically. We have the power to set a vision for the kids and teachers and make it happen. We have the power to communicate the vision in unique ways. We have the power to motivate our teachers and students by taking the time to get to know each and every one of them as best we can. ***Common sense leadership will never go wrong. Hop on the Clue Bus...the more of you we get on the bus, the better off we will be and the more success stories we will read.***

I find myself communicating with parents through notes, emails and post cards about their kids' successes. I also find myself thanking parents for all they do for their children...here's why:

Communication & Motivation

DW DUBUQUE WAHLERT Golden Eagle Volleyball

2005 KANE ST.
DUBUQUE, IOWA 52001

Tom Keating
Head Coach
W (319) 583-9771
Fax 319-583-9775
H (319) 557-1366

Assistants:
Jim Kuhl
Jan Thyne
Deb Norman

Gene Pierotti
Athletic Director

Don Miller
Principal

State
Tournament
Appearances

1973
1974
1976
1977
1978
1981
1982
1985
1986
1987
1989
1990
1991
1992
1993

November 14, 1993

Dear Dave and Linda,

Just a short note to let you know how much I've truly enjoyed the opportunity to work with Heidy these past three years. She has been a credit to Wahlert Volleyball and a credit to Wahlert High School.

Without a doubt, Heidy is the best leader I've had in my coaching career. I've had players who've collected more awards and accolades, but I've never had a young lady who was so willing to give her time and effort to her teammates. Heidy is one of the few athletes I know who is capable of putting her own concerns aside for the sake of her team.

As captain, Heidy did a remarkable job of keeping this team focused on what was important. It was no accident that we were able to succeed despite the differences in age and interests of our players. Heidy did everything in her power to make sure that each player felt she was an important part of this group.

We've all seen what a terrific player Heidy has become. What I am more impressed with, however, is the type of person Heidy has become. Never in my career have I had a player I was more willing to trust. Heidy knows the difference between right and wrong. She has made the choice to do what's right. That, as we know, is not always the popular choice. As a result, Heidy is one of the best role models to ever come through the Wahlert program. Our younger players truly admire and respect her. She has had a tremendous impact on them.

I think I've seen enough high school students and coached enough athletes to know that they don't turn out the way they do by accident. Heidy is who she is, in large part, because of the way you've raised her. As they say, "The nut doesn't fall far from the tree." Heidy is lucky to have parents who care enough about her to set rules she must live by. She is lucky to have parents who care enough about her to support her in all she does. And I want you to know that she appreciates you.

I want to thank you personally for all you've done for the Wahlert Volleyball program these past four years. Whether it was pizza at Shot Tower, an encouraging word when I needed it, food at a tournament, or a "Go Blue!" at just the right time, I truly appreciate you help.

Thank you so much for choosing to send Heidy to Wahlert. My experience with her has had a tremendous impact on my life. She has taught me a great deal about trust, commitment, hard work and persistence. I miss her already.

Sincerely,

Tom

Tom Keating

State Champions   1974 '76 '77 '78 '86 '87 '90 '91 '92
MVC Champions   1978 '79 '81 '83 '85 '86 '87 '89 '90 '91 '92

I am the Master of my Fate and the Captain of my Soul. You are too...

IV

High Expectations with Human Touch

CLUE BUS NOTE #4

High expectations + consistent and supportive leadership = success

[suh k-**ses**] success: noun - the favorable or prosperous termination of attempts or endeavors; the accomplishment of one's goals.

To me, there is little separation between my work and my personal life. I am who I am, regardless if it's a weekday during the school year, or a weekend day at home. My positive outlook is the same for my staff as it is for my family. I also share the fact that I am a human being, just like everyone else. At home, my family lives on the phrases, "The most important thing in the world is family," and "Be Awesome!" At school, we live on two phrases, "Our job is to make each day the very best day for every child," and "You are a professional. Just do it and do it well." The messages deliver the same expectations. Be the best you can be and take care of each other,

High Expectations with Human Touch

every day, no matter what. If that attitude is in place **and modeled**, the school environment will thrive.

Common sense leadership tells us that our personality and attitude about humanity leak through in everything that we do. Teachers know leaders who talk the talk and also know those who walk the walk. Period. If you talk with no action, it will have a dramatic impact on the culture of your school or organization. Leaders must keep their word. People are relying on you and looking up to you for guidance and feedback. What we say is sacred to some. That sounds awfully pretentious, but it's not meant to be...it is simply the truth. People learn to love us or hate us and it really depends on how we treat them and how we package information. Students, teachers and athletes look up to good leaders. They want to impress them. They don't want to let them down. They want badly to improve and be recognized in the eyes of their leader. So what are you waiting for? Tell your best teachers how amazing they are. Recognize them and their efforts. Guide them to take leadership roles and go above and beyond to help kids grow. If they are working hard and hear it from you, I guarantee they will work even harder!

On the flip side, talk to those who are not living up to the expectations. <u>Do not be afraid to do so.</u> Helping those who struggle will make your school stronger and will grow the respect others have for you. There is nothing more degrading than the leader who writes "Excellent" evaluations for everyone. That's like a slap in the face to those who excel. Having difficult conversations with teachers is not easy. Following through on helping teachers who need improvement isn't easy. ***Common sense tells us that holding yourself and others to high expectations isn't easy either, but since when is good work easy?*** I encourage you to keep documentation on all of your teachers, but especially those who struggle. Student success depends on what kinds of teachers are in front of them. In my experience, <u>**effective teachers**</u> are motivated, determined, self-starters, responsible, leaders, problem solvers, team players, committed, fair, focused, passionate, nurturing, mature and possess a stellar work ethic. When you look at evaluating teachers, there are several things that stand out in excellent teachers. Not only do their students grow each year, but these teachers grow in their profession as well. They take constructive criticism and turn it into success. The most important quality in a successful teacher is their *attitude*. So many times excellent teachers will ask how they can improve. Sometimes I respond by saying that as long as your attitude and work ethic stay where they are, you will always improve and grow. We've all seen them... the teachers who go above and beyond. They are amazing and it shows in every aspect of evaluation. With that said, common sense tells us that not everyone is excellent. Leaders who have and model high expectations must do what it takes to get the best teachers in front of students every day. I take it upon myself to observe in classrooms frequently and offer feedback to discuss. I also take it upon myself to hold people to what is expected. Like I said earlier, we are professionals. Just do it and do it well. If you don't, why bother?

I've worked with many principals who didn't spend a lot of time in classrooms. They would write evaluations at the last minute and hand them to teachers as they walked out the door for summer break. What is that? The whole point behind observation is to help teachers GROW. We all have the potential to be better and common sense leadership is a huge part of that. <u>The best part of an evaluation cycle is the conversations I have with teachers</u>. It is so awesome to hear teachers talk about what they want to see in their classroom and I get to be a part of helping get them there. Cool stuff! This can be done! It takes a lot of time, but it is so worth it. Observing teachers and talking to them about their goals and student achievement is the best part of leadership. Having high expectations, helping teachers set goals and guiding them is such a powerful thing, yet it isn't done enough. If you want to make a true difference, set high expectations and live by them. Have empathy for people, but hold them accountable. Be real. Real people laugh.

I love to laugh. Wrapped up inside this principal in nice clothes is the biggest smart ass you will ever meet. I often share that side through jokes and comics in memos and newsletters with staff. It is relationship building that allows many funny things to be said and talked about at school. Our jobs are stressful. They are crazy and they are awesome. Laughter is the best medicine when it comes to stress relief and building positive school culture.

Together we deal with so many funny stories because we are dealing with kids. Kids say the funniest things and sharing those stories helps build relationships with each other. Keeping things on the lighter side helps with everything. No matter what mandate is next or what report is due, taking things in stride with a side of laughter goes a long way. Common sense tells us that people will feel comfortable sharing stories about kids when they feel safe to do so. Laughing together is an excellent way to let people know

High Expectations with Human Touch

you are down to earth and a person who likes to have fun. *You are leading with human touch.* Leaders who don't have fun with their colleagues close doors to relationships and trust. It's kind of like classroom management. Once you have established & modeled the expectations and worked on building trust, it's okay to let loose a little. Remember, part of helping people grow is showing that you are a regular person. Why do some leaders put themselves on a pedestal? It doesn't work well that way. **Leaders who can relate to and talk with people are the most successful.** Leaders who have difficulty breaking through the barrier and can't laugh with their colleagues will have a hard time. *On the Clue Bus, we have vision, passion and we are clear that people come first...*

I feel extremely fortunate to work in a district where a great deal of common sense exists. Class sizes are small and that is something held in high regard in our community. You can get to know every student well. You can help every student grow socially, emotionally and academically. What could be better? I also understand the reality of high class size and the frustration it can bring. It's interesting that, as teachers and leaders, the expectations are the same regardless of the number of students in your class. The biggest group I taught was 42 seventh grade math students. My smallest class was 29 and it was like a dream. Think about how much time you can spend with 29 versus 42. <u>It's truly common sense</u>.

As leaders with high expectations regardless of numbers or other excuses, find the time to have the human touch. Just as excellent doctors have stellar bedside manner, common sense leaders lead with human touch. Help when you can. Schedule creatively to make time for teams to meet. Listen when they need to be heard. Cover a class once in a while. Play music at the end of the day and invite them to dance in the hallways. Tell a joke on the intercom. Cancel a meeting when the team is tired or it's the first day of beautiful weather. There are many things we can do as leaders to ease the stress of the very difficult job of teaching students, yet honor high expectations. I hold myself to the very highest standards and expect that of others as well, however, at the forefront of my actions is leading with human touch. Life is short. Enjoy the people in your building. Enjoy the families. Enjoy the students. It's worth all of the time you spend. ***Leading with human touch is a very important aspect of Common Sense Leadership!***

V

Compassion

CLUE BUS NOTE #5

Taking a walk in someone else's shoes is worth every step

[kuh m-pash-uh n] compassion: adjective - a feeling of deep sympathy and sorrow for another who is stricken by misfortune, accompanied by a strong desire to alleviate the suffering.

Standing in the principal's office, as her assistant, I will never forget the day when a teacher came in looking very upset. She said that she needed to call her husband because she was actively having a miscarriage. This was a teacher who had been at the school for a long time. She and her husband were having trouble getting pregnant and they were so excited that they finally were. The poor woman could hardly speak, but was trying to ask if someone could cover her class so she could call her husband. I told her no problem, that I would help her. The principal told her to go to her car, call her

Compassion

husband and come back in to teach. I was sick about that. It was 1:30 in the afternoon and this woman was going through a personal tragedy. I walked out of the office with her and told her to go home. I told her not to worry that I would cover her class for the rest of the day and that's what I did. I saw no other option.

I feel very strongly that walking in someone else's shoes and feeling what they may feel is very powerful. ***Being a common sense leader means taking care of your people.*** It means having compassion for their lives outside of school. We have and will continue to have so many opportunities to simply show love and compassion for people. When I was an assistant principal, we had a first grade student named Abigail whose neuroblastoma was in remission. She was the cutest little thing. Her therapy left her with wispy thin hair and hearing aids. Her mother was and is on the board of the American Childhood Cancer Association and showed me a fundraiser called Pjammin for Kids with Cancer. She asked if I would think about running the fundraiser and I couldn't wait to get started! Can you imagine having a child with cancer? Running a fundraiser at school is the LEAST I could do to show kindness and compassion. It is now a tradition at that school to host Pjammin for Kids with Cancer to show support in fighting the disease! Compassion for people is an outstanding way to build the culture and climate of your school. This year, that student celebrated seven years cancer-free!

Dealing with people means dealing with death in families. It means dealing with teachers getting sick and taking leaves. It comes with sharing news with the staff that isn't always pleasant. Leaders are truly in powerful places. We deliver the good and the bad. We deliver happiness and sadness. The way in which we do so has a HUGE impact on our school and always will. It is when people are at their worst that they remember who you were to them. Were you an obstacle or a teammate? My job as a common sense leader is to take away any obstacle that gets in the way of teaching and learning. My job is to be a partner, a teammate and a friend at times.

My beautiful friend and old neighbor Shannon, lost her little girl to cancer two years ago. Leah and my son, Garrett went to preschool together and were the best of friends. Leah told everyone in the neighborhood that she was going to marry Garrett. She was so proud and so was Garrett. Their friendship was so innocent and special. They would read together at school and put their arms around each other. Shannon is a teacher who had an amazing support group at her school. Her teaching colleagues helped her through so many difficult times. Think about the impact you have as a leader when tragedies strike your building. You can help. You can listen. You can make heartfelt efforts to encourage and strengthen the bonds of others. If you are on the Clue Bus, you know what to do when people are struggling. I am very thankful that many were on the bus at Shannon's school. Leah became an angel on 12-12-12 and I often feel that she waited for the stars to align for her. Shannon's empathetic and supportive colleagues do an annual fundraiser in honor of Leah. They get it.

I had an amazing paraprofessional who took in her pre-teenage cousin because her aunt was very sick and couldn't take care of her. This woman already had a small child at home and thought nothing of taking in her cousin so she could have a good life. When

Compassion

the time came for her aunt to pass, she stepped up even more gaining custody of the girl. Imagine the unselfishness. When her aunt was dying, she would feel terrible missing school and would worry about her students. I told her to never worry and to take care of herself and her family. I asked our staff to make donations for her and sent her a gift card telling her to use it to help ease the pain. When people are hurting and stressed, a little grocery money can go a long way. Anything to help ease the burden life brings to us at times.

When I was 22, my mother was diagnosed with colon cancer. She underwent years of treatment and fought the fight like nobody's business. I would go visit her almost every weekend and sometimes take Friday afternoons off to make the three hour drive back home. It was difficult being away from her. I will never forget getting my final evaluation that showed "needs improvement" in attendance because I was only present 95% of the time. Talk about lack of compassion. I was so mad about that because that leader never walked a minute in my shoes. It felt as if she didn't care. It felt as if she went on with her life as if nothing mattered and she showed no compassion to me. As a leader, I have learned to differentiate. You see, calling in sick for no good reason and being at school 95% of the time is one thing, but leaving half days to take care of your sick mother is another. Just like teachers have to differentiate in the classroom, common sense leaders have to differentiate as well. Fair isn't everyone getting the same thing. Fair is everyone getting what they need in order to be successful.

I made the trip a million times until I got pregnant with my first child and could no longer travel. Four weeks after Lilly was born, my mom was rushed to the Mayo Clinic in Rochester, Minnesota because they couldn't stop her bleeding. I bundled up my first born child and drove to see my mom. It was there in her hospital room that she looked me in the eye and said she was going to die. There I was, a new mom listening to my mom tell me that the end was near. My heart was just sick. I stayed in a hotel with Lilly for two weeks. After that, my mom was transferred back home and was put on hospice. Lilly and I moved back home and my husband would come visit us on the weekends. My maternity leave was up and we decided that I would ask for a longer leave so I could help my mom die. That sounds terrible, but those who have had a terminal parent, know what I mean.

Back at school during this time, I had one parent on the board tell the principal that she needed to stop hiring the "young chick-a-dees that get pregnant and extend their maternity leave." Her son was in my fourth grade class that year. Wow. Selfish. Sad. Rude. Far from compassionate. That mother went on to nominate me for a Golden Apple Award for Teaching Excellence. Interesting how she thought I was such a great teacher for her son, but didn't possess the compassion to look at me as a person, a mother, and a grieving daughter. On April 18, 2004, the day I was to report back to school, my mother passed away. No card from my school. No flowers at her funeral. I was going through the greatest tragedy of my young life and the leadership did not walk in my shoes.

Something to think about...

VI
Organization

CLUE BUS NOTE #6

If you want united action, you must be organized.

[awr-g*uh*-nahyz] organize: verb -to form as or into a whole consisting of interdependent or coordinated parts, especially for united action

Common sense leadership represents organization in many ways. Leading people effectively means that you, as the captain, have to know where you are going and have an idea & vision of how you are going to get there. Once there, you must have a plan to grow and change with the time, the people, the demands and the generation. Being organized means, in your thoughts and words, both verbal and written, you have cohesive thoughts and plans. You express them in a positive, honest and confident manner. You make people believe in you. You make people want to follow you and create a sense of

Organization

curiosity in them. Organized leaders with common sense never lose their curiosity. They never grow old in their thoughts. They never allow their minds to get stale. They gain momentum and energy from others motivated to be the best and, in turn, motivate others to give their very best.

Organization starts with core beliefs. It is when core beliefs are established that organized thoughts can start. When organized thoughts are in place, written plans can begin. After written plans are drafted, the fun begins! Common sense tells us to create a vison and leadership style based on all that we have read, what we truly believe and what we have experienced. Every leader has a different set of core beliefs and execution plan for those beliefs. ***However, leaders on the Clue Bus have a balance of confidence and humbleness about them.*** You see, the best laid plans are not effective if no one believes in you.

Several years ago, during a professional development session, I was asked to write down my core beliefs. At the time, it seemed like such a daunting task, overwhelming to think about. Turns out, it was one of the most beneficial and valuable exercises I have even been asked to do. In fact, I find myself visiting that list often and streamlining my thoughts and actions to those core beliefs. Writing down what I truly thought about leadership and life began the organization of my thoughts and vision of not only who I was, but where they would take me.

Here is what I wrote:

My Core Beliefs:

- Honesty – even when it is difficult
- Compassion – walk in other people's shoes before making decisions
- Work Ethic – high expectations for self and others
- Communicate – people who don't know can only assume
- Appreciate – recognize greatness and appreciate it
- All Kids Can Learn – regardless of what life has dealt, make it better for every child
- Humor – laugh, motivate, make it real

I think about and refer back to these beliefs often. If you are going to be true to yourself and a common sense leader, you have to have a strong belief system of who you are, what you stand for and how you do business. Without a strong sense of self, how can you lead?

Everything I do involves my core beliefs; the way I talk, the way I communicate, the way I motivate and the way I carry & organize myself. Most every teacher wants to do his/her best. They have very full plates each day and night. Their jobs don't end at 3:00 PM. They are planning lessons, buying supplies, grading papers and creating projects well into the night. Trusting that they are putting forth the necessary effort to be successful, common sense tells me to take away any possible barriers to their success. Being an organized leader is the number one barrier that can be taken away. How can a teacher feel organized if their leader is not organized?

Organization

Leaders chasing the Clue Bus never catch it because they can't follow it. They get lost and confused which causes their teachers to get lost and confused. This common sense chain now continues to the student. Imagine their learning environment when leaders and teachers are confused. Lack of organization equates to lack of progress and growth.

Written communication is vital to common sense organization. Just like Goldilocks was trying to find the "just right" items, common sense leaders need to find the "just right" amount of communication. I provide a monthly calendar to my staff, as well as a weekly memo reviewing the week's events, meetings and reminders. Often in the weekly memos you can find a funny cartoon related to the most recent events. You can find quotes to think about, articles to read for professional development or shout outs to staff members. You can find examples of these weekly memos on my website – www.hoponthecluebus.com. In all that I produce, my core beliefs are expressed and you will see a pattern of that consistent belief system in the forms I use.

Another very important part of organization is establishing consistency. What do the memos look like? What can teachers expect? When can they expect the memos? Being upfront and establishing consistent communication guidelines will ease the expectation because question marks are removed. There is nothing worse than the unknown. The unknown often brings feelings that are overthought and boil over into unnecessary issues and drama that you don't have time for. I do everything I can to avoid unnecessary drama…I already spent four years in high school.

Organization

My goal is always to have teachers working on their art of teaching. I find it my job to make sure they have the science of teaching. I am responsible to get them curriculum, materials, supplies and professional development. I am responsible for helping guide teachers through data and make decisions, much like a teacher guiding her students with modeling and then a gradual release. The goal is to make students independent thinkers and that goal is no different for my teachers.

   Organize your thoughts...
      Organize your words...
         Know who you are and get on the bus!

VII

Evaluation

CLUE BUS NOTE #7

Evaluation is about convincing people to think about their practice and providing support so they understand that growth is part of being human.

> **[grohth]** growth: noun - the act or process, or a manner of growing; development; gradual increase.

Evaluation is a difficult concept for many. Some people take it very personally and others take it as a challenge to improve. At the end of the day, evaluation should be a process where both the principal and teacher work together toward a goal. All of us have areas we could improve. What makes the difference is how that need for growth is approached.

Effective evaluation boils down to trust and relationships. If you don't trust your leader, you won't let your guard down to discuss areas

Evaluation

of improvement. Instead, most people get defensive and angry because they don't feel their leader is listening. Taking the time and effort to accurately evaluate people is very hard work, even overwhelming at times. However, effective, fair and accurate evaluations will be held in the highest regard in your school.

At the beginning of my career, I worked at a Catholic School in Chicago for one year. The principal visited my classroom one time that year. She came for a 15 minute observation the day before spring break. Ask any teacher what kids are like the day before spring break, the day before winter break or the two weeks before summer. They are like caged animals waiting to get out. In all honesty, so are the teachers! I didn't care when she observed me, in fact, I have always told my administrators to come in whenever they'd like, because they would be exposed to the same high expectations and engagement in my classroom. My students were great during the observation and I thought things went well. At my post conference, three weeks later, she told me that she didn't like that I had a coffee pot in my classroom because it was against the school rules. She also said that I should dress better. I was taken back by this for several reasons. At 23 years of age, I had never drank a cup of coffee, hence the fact that the coffee pot was not in my room, but in the room of the teacher next door to me. Although I explained that to her, she still wrote it up on my final evaluation. Getting paid $21,000 a year and trying to afford an apartment in the city, I didn't have suits and fancy dresses at that time in my life. I wore khakis and collared shirts. I looked casual and professional. It was hard to swallow coming from a woman who wore large dresses, nylons and Birkenstocks each day. In conclusion of that experience, she did nothing to help grow my teaching skills. The most important thing about evaluation is that it is a tool to grow. I guess it worked in the long run because I now love coffee and wear suits and fancy dresses to school!

Common sense leaders celebrate the strengths in their teachers and help develop areas in need of improvement. The most amazing part of evaluation is conversation. Teachers are smart people. Most of them know where they need to improve or step it up. It is the job of a common sense leader to help teachers feel comfortable saying they need to improve or need help in certain areas.

Along with inaccurate evaluations come the ghost evaluations. I also worked at a school where evaluations appeared out of thin air and were handed to the teacher on the way out the door on the last day of school. No discussion. No goals. Nothing. This helped me learn the difference between compliance and dedicated work. You see, some teachers may be fine with no discussion, no goals and no growth observation. Others, however, work hard, are effective and want the chance to talk about their practice. Evaluation is about everything in this book. It is about relationships, listening, understanding, high expectations, work ethic, culture and being organized.

Being an effective evaluator is not an easy task. Working hard to get into classrooms as much as possible with the tremendous amount of other tasks, is overwhelming. Gathering evidence is the best way to write a fair and appropriate evaluation. Guiding your teachers to understand what evidence means is half the battle. Helping people understand that this evaluation is not about <u>YOU</u>, but it is about

Evaluation

YOUR PRACTICE. The best message I give to teachers is that YOU can grow in your PRACTICE and I will help you. Enter those with their guards up. This is where evaluations take a turn. This is where you learn the most about your teachers. Will they listen and reflect on their practice or will they be defensive and upset. We have both in our schools. The difficult ones in defense mode are draining. The positive, self-reflecting ones are inspirational. I find honor in helping each, but also knowing that in the end, I know which one will find success.

As Mr. Keating told us – I am the Master of my Fate and the Captain of my Soul.

Every teacher sets his or her path with attitude…
I just act as the guidance for individual and team growth…

VIII

Relationships

CLUE BUS NOTE #8

If people don't have trust in you, forget it.

[truhst] trust: noun - reliance on the integrity, strength, ability, surety, etc., of a person or thing; confidence.

Building relationships with people is the **MOST** important part of leadership. People can see through bullshit. When I meet someone, I can tell within five minutes if that person is full of it. That feeling is hard to get rid of as the conversation continues. We've all been there. You have a boss or colleague who you just don't trust. Think about it. Think about who they are, how they talk and what you feel about their character. It is impossible to work with people you do not trust. ***Common Sense Leaders work in many ways to build trusting relationships.*** Trusting relationships are the foundation to any successful opportunity.

Relationships

Building trust with people starts with integrity and character. A common sense leader never forgets the steps he/she took to be where he/she is…A common sense leader is in the classroom learning and growing with the teacher. A common sense leader talks *with* people, not *at* people. A common sense leader works to get to know the person behind the teaching and realizes that teachers are mothers, fathers, students, widows, novice, seasoned, etc. There is a story behind every person who works in your building. Building trusting relationships will allow you to get to know the real person behind the teaching mask. People act certain ways for a reason. Life throws some pretty tough things at people. Understanding your teachers and their journeys may help you gain perspective into why they do what they do and say what they say. Leadership is unique in that you have to differentiate how you lead. <u>The more you learn about your teachers, the better you can facilitate their growth.</u> New teachers need guidance in a different way than veteran teachers. There are also times when the new teachers outshine the veterans and usually it has to do with attitude or fearlessness. New teachers come to us fresh, excited and ready to change the world. Some new teachers come to us too eager and offend the veteran…enter the common sense leader. What an opportunity to build relationships with people. When you talk to them and listen to them and keep your word, the trusting relationship grows and grows. It takes time and effort, but it is so worth every minute. Think about how hard it is to have those difficult conversations about performance and attitude…if you build relationships with people, they aren't quite as difficult.

On a daily basis, I deal with situations that need trusting relationships in order to be successful. On top of creating schedules, talking with parents, evaluating teachers, participating in and presenting at meetings, printing and studying student data and trying to get a bite to eat during lunch, a leader deals with this…

- A teacher came to my office in tears telling me that she is sorry if she doesn't seem herself, but that she is getting a divorce and trying to make it as easy as she can for her kids.
- A secretary had to leave school and fly to Florida to take care of her father who was in the hospital ready to die.
- A library clerk's father passed. She couldn't talk, just had to leave.
- A teacher needed to leave because she just found out that her baby stopped growing at seven weeks, although she was 14 weeks along.
- A teacher came in asking to leave because his daughter was running a high fever and was lethargic at day care.
- When meeting with a struggling teacher, he cried stating, "Everything I do is hard for me. I have had many jobs and failed and now I feel like I am failing with my teaching."
- Kids fighting on the playground.
- An early morning phone call from a teacher to tell me that her daughter passed away the night before and asked that we pray for her daughter's soul.
- Bloody noses, scrapped knees, seizures
- Phone calls about too much homework or too little homework

The list is endless and if relationships are not built, it makes all of these situations much more difficult to deal with. I have worked with leaders who do not make life easier for their people because of the decisions they make. Some see teachers as teachers and nothing

Relationships

else. The truth is our job or career is a <u>part</u> of who we are, a big part. ***But Common Sense Leadership sees beyond the job and into the person.*** People have lives, feelings, emotions and at the end of the day most people just want to do well. Leaders have the responsibility and opportunity to help make people successful.

I also believe very strongly that building relationships involves opening up your life to those you work with. I am open about the difficulties of juggling motherhood with a career. I am open with the stress, love and joy of raising children. I have seen the magic of people feeling comfortable just because they share that I put my pants on each morning just as they do. (Although why it is that the size keeps growing if I never get the chance to sit down to eat lunch? Hmm.) The key to building relationships with people is to be open, honest and humble. Talking with people about the stress of life, sharing their fears and accomplishments is powerful. ***I often look at my job as an opportunity to make life for people a little easier at times.*** Life is hard enough and you don't need a leader making it harder.

Those types of leaders are certainly out there though. Leaders who are not on the Clue Bus. Those who focus on the wrong things. Those who don't really care about people. Those who demand - those who expect respect - those who don't listen. Unfortunately, there are a lot of leaders out there who are not using common sense. Leaders who don't build trust lead schools where frustration is high, teachers are salty and climate & culture are sour. Not good. Not productive. Not Common Sense Leadership.

IX

It's Up to You

CLUE BUS NOTE #9

Reflecting on who you are and what you do is powerful. It's never too late to make a change for the better.

[ri-**flekt**] reflect: verb - to think, ponder, or meditate

Well, it's up to you. You can join me on the Clue Bus, or you can stand at the bus stop. Those on the Clue Bus make things happen. They set goals & high expectations and guide their teachers to success. They sacrifice time and energy for the good of their teams and most of all lead by example. <u>Those on the Clue Bus make a difference each and every day</u>. As you reflect on your leadership style, think about who you are. Think about your core beliefs. If you have never taken a moment to write out your core beliefs, do so. It is a very powerful mental organization of your thoughts. As I tell my own children, your mind will believe whatever you tell it. If your true core beliefs are at the forefront of all that you do, your leadership will thrive. You, as a leader, will grow more than ever if you are on that organized path. Reflecting on your practice is vital to your growth.

I asked all of the faculty and staff that I have ever worked with to write a paragraph describing what, in their eyes, makes an effective leader. I asked that they add their position and age to see if there is a difference in what novice and veteran teachers want in a leader. Here are the results:

<u>Kindergarten Teacher</u>, *50 years old*
In my many years of teaching, I have come to realize that administrators can choose to look for the negative or look for the positive in each teacher. If you look hard enough, you can find something negative about any one of us. After all, we are human. However, it only takes a moment to see many good characteristics in teachers. Teachers all have strengths that can be shared with others. We don't all have to be excellent at everything. We simply need to be excellent at sharing what we are excellent at! We all strive to do our best in a positive, supportive environment with an administrator that believes in all we can be and continue to strive to be. A motivating, supportive administrator encourages teachers to grow professionally among peers. Teachers who feel supported will naturally be motivated and therefore motivate their students and teach with excellence. We all choose to educate students in order to truly make a difference. Why then wouldn't an administrator choose to provide a positive atmosphere with productive teamwork? After all, it only takes a brief moment to see the positive in every one of us!

<u>Digital Literacy Teacher</u>, *30 years old*
A good leader supports me and trusts me to do the job I was hired to do. A good leader is present and leads by example. A good leader delegates and isn't afraid to ask for help when he or she doesn't know

the answer. A good leader inspires me to be a better educator. A good leader cultivates a positive work environment and encourages collaboration. The knowledge that my leader has the aforementioned traits allows me to take risks, thus, growing my students in and out of the classroom. A great leader motivates me to arrive each day with a smile and makes me want to be the best educator I can be. Even if *I* can't accomplish something; I know *we* can!

Language Arts teacher, 43 years old
This type of leader encourages and even at times when necessary, *insists* that teachers plan, plan, and plan some more. Good teachers can "wing it," but even those most seasoned teachers do a better job when they are required to write detailed lesson plans and be accountable for what is going on in their classroom each day. When given too much freedom, even the best of workers (in any job) will slack. An effective leader has somewhat high expectations for those he/she leads. In addition, an effective leader shows appreciation for hard work which encourages more hard work and reciprocal appreciation. Lastly, an effective leader delegates rather than micromanaging.

Junior High Science Teacher, 39 years old
Having worked under five principals, I have had different experiences. I grew as a teacher the most under the leadership of one principal. During this time, I felt like my grade level and principal were part of a team with a clear vision. When we met, we discussed curriculum and how to best get things done—and we took action. Moreover, we all held each other in the highest respect and felt like family. As a family, we supported and encouraged each other to try new things or find new strategies. With her hard work and enthusiasm, you wanted to be part of her team.

It's Up to You

Kindergarten Teacher, 27 years old
A leader works to support and encourage all those around her. She helps by offering guidance, a fresh perspective and new ideas. With a unique way of approaching teaching, a leader can inspire change in other educators around her. By "shaking things up", a leader once guided me to revamp my English Language Arts and guided reading curriculum. After doing so, my students were more engaged learners and had a better understanding of our standards. It was AWESOME to see! Leaders encourage you to work that much harder to see results and it makes the growth even more rewarding!

6th grade teacher, 46 years old
The most important characteristic I find in a leader that helps me be the very best teacher I can be is the ability to listen. If I am going to this leader - there is a really strong reason. I need to be heard. From that listening there can be all sorts of angles: empathy, advice, guidance but this needs to be done in a professional/respectful manner. And if I am out of line/wrong, tell me. I will work hard on fixing it. The best leaders lead by example. If you want me to do something, the leader also needs to be doing it. Most leaders come from the classroom and work their way up. There are a lot of new responsibilities that make a leader forget what it was like dealing with the day-to-day "petty classroom things" that wear a teacher down. What seems like no big deal might take a lot of my time to complete. If I am spending time on the paperwork, the students suffer. When I am at the end of my rope, step in and help me. I obviously need it. These are the things that will then trickle down to the students and make me a better teacher, and therefore them, better students - socially, emotionally or academically.

Grade 5 Teacher, 39 years old
A good leader has many qualities, but patience, confidence, effective communication, and drive stand out to me. Also, someone who is constantly growing and evolving themselves makes a good leader. If you see their drive and motivation, it pushes you to keep moving and growing and doing your best. Other characteristics include being passionate and supportive. Good leaders state clear expectations and communicate their vision with their staff. I also think having high expectations (within reason) is important because it promotes growth and crushes stagnancy.

These qualities can all be transferred into the classroom with students. Having high expectations placed upon me, causes me to have high expectations with my students. Being patient, passionate about teaching, and communicating clearly and effectively hopefully influences my students positively. If students see me working hard and valuing growth and learning, then hopefully that will translate into something meaningful in their educational career.

Special Education Teacher, 54 years old and still learning
The characteristics that I find in a leader who helps me to be the very best teacher are: power, vision, trust; someone who guides and directs; someone who works well under stress and deadlines; someone who has self confidence and the ability to project this confidence on others building their trust and commitment. I feel a good leader focuses on shared decision making and teamwork. This leader conveys a sense of leadership to teachers who in turn projects this on their students and provides them the opportunity to assume leadership roles in their lives in and out of the classroom.

Classroom Teacher, 37 years old
I believe effective principals set standards and expectations, but also allow freedom and art in how those expectations and standards are met. When the standards are set there is no room for uncertainty. As a leader the principal encourages the teachers to achieve and exceed the expectations using the individual teacher strengths, the collaborative strengths of the staff, and also provides opportunities for professional growth and development in areas which need further refinement. It is important that the principal build a strong, POSITIVE community. Often the teachers have established communities with peers, or grade level partners. It is a principal who provides the foundations of an entire school community. The school environment needs to be welcoming and warm for the staff and the students. Effective principals develop positive relationships with the staff as a whole and each teacher individually. I believe positive attitudes towards growth and development allow students to grow. Recognizing the small successes, as well as, the large ones is an important factor in developing students. The principal should create positive relationships with the students. The students need to know and see the principal as a part of their educational journey. The children need to be encouraged by the principal and the principal should recognize successes (whether it be by note, comment on report card, or speaking with the child). I believe the principal should encourage and celebrate growth as a student in academics and growth as a person in their character. It is important that the teachers and principal promote lifelong learners through curriculum, experiences and a sense of community.

Early Childhood Special Education Teacher, 48 years old
I can be the very best teacher that I can be when I work with a leader that shares a mutual respect with me. I automatically have a certain

level of respect for my leader because of her position, her education, and her experience. That respect will grow over time as we work together. I understand that my leader and I will not always agree, but we must be respectful of our individual positions. At the same time, I expect to be treated with a certain level of respect because of my position, education, and experience. The respect that I receive from my leader fosters an environment of collaboration with her. We can discuss matters, both big and small, and know that we both want a solution that is appropriate. Ultimately, we share a common goal and our ability to work together professionally allows me to accomplish all that I need to do.

Grade 4 Teacher, 36 years old
A leader that listens is a very important quality to have. I want a leader that truly listens to my concerns, fears, struggles, ideas and celebrations. When a leader does that, I feel valued and that my job matters.

Reading Specialist, 35 years old
A leader that helps me be my best is a person who provides the structure and environment that allows for collaboration and teamwork with colleagues and provides the time, resources and information I need to help my students. Someone who has an open door policy for conversations with staff and is realistic and understanding about life both in and outside of school helps as well.

6-8 General/Vocal Music Teacher, 53 years old
I find that a person who backs me up when dealing with students, especially with discipline issues, helps me to be an effective teacher. This is particularly important when in front of the students. An

effective leader would talk with me privately if they had an issue with the way I handled things and give me constructive (not condescending) suggestions on ways to handle the situation differently in the future. I also would like a leader to acknowledge and appreciate the work that is put into a lesson or activity.

Art Teacher Grades K-8, 44 years old
I think that leaders must lead by example. If we want students to trust us enough to confide in us and help the "whole child" grow, (which gives them confidence in their learning), leaders must find ways to build trust with these students as well. They need to not be afraid to let children know that they are humans that make mistakes too. They hurt and feel joy just like they do. They need to show balance. "All work and no play makes Johnny a dull boy!" If a leader brings fun (for everyone, not just a select few) to the workplace, I feel you are more inclined to respond when it's time to get serious and get work done!

Middle School Teacher, 36 Years Young
Leaders are in a sense coaches. A good coach prepares you for the task at hand. When you face adversity, a good coach recognizes your struggle and provides you the knowledge, skill, and opportunity to overcome that struggle. In addition, win or lose, a good coach acknowledges your effort and commitment to the program and understands that we are in this as a team. This allows me to translate my coaching onto the students.

4th Grade Teacher, 54 years old
What I find the best in a leader would be compassion and fairness. I rank

It's Up to You

compassion first because an understanding leader with compassion would motivate me to change or stride for higher understanding in my field. As humans, we need understanding and a connection to a leader. I like a leader who is committed to guidance and leadership to get me on the right path to be the best teacher I can be.

Assistant Principal, 36 years old
Characteristics that I find in a leader who helps me to be the very best I can be include being a good listener when I have doubts, being supportive when I need encouragement and being the safety net between me and parents when needed. The leader who has these characteristics allows for student growth in and out of the classroom because the teacher feels supported and confident in what they are doing and instill those feelings into their students.

Here it is in black and white. They are sharing what they need from us. Listen to them. Go make a difference. No questions, no complaints, no excuses. Just do it and do it well. Be awesome. I hope you decide to join me on the Clue Bus. You **CAN** and **WILL** make a difference if you take a seat. All the best on your common sense journey!

Visit me at: www.hoponthecluebus.com

About the Author

I'd like to tell you about the author of this book, my mom. She is a loving, caring, encouraging and awesome mom. She comes home every day and asks us about our days. She is very supportive to me and my brothers. My mom attends all of our school events and sporting activities. She tells us that the most important thing is family and to never give up. Every time we get out of the car, she tells us to have good manners, to have fun and to do your best. My mom is the best mom I could ever have! – Lilly LaFleur, Age 11